Also by David Miller:

Thesis, hawkhaven press, San Francisco, *forthcoming*

Spiritual Letters (Series 2, #1-5), with artwork by Denis Mizzi, NYX Press, Sydney (Australia), 2001

Commentaries (II), Runaway Spoon Press, Port Charlotte, Florida, 2000

The Dark Path, tel-let, Charleston, Illinois, 2000

Commentaries, tel-let, 1999

Spiritual Letters (1-12), hawkhaven press, 1999

The ABCs of Robert Lax (ed., with Nicholas Zurbrugg), Stride, Exeter (UK), 1999

Art and Disclosure: Seven Essays, Stride, 1998

Darkness Enfolding: A Story, tel-let, 1998

Collected Poems, University of Salzburg Press, Salzburg (Austria), 1997

Appearance & Event, paradigm press, Providence, 1997

Stromata, Burning Deck Press, Providence, 1995

True Points, Spectacular Diseases Press, Peterborough (UK), 1992

Pictures of Mercy, Stride, 1991

W.H. Hudson and the Elusive Paradise, Macmillan, London / St. Martins Press, NY, 1990

Losing to Compassion, Origin Press, Kyoto (Japan), 1985

Unity, Singing Horse Press, Blue Bell, Pennsylvania, 1981

Primavera, Burning Deck Press, 1979

David Miller

The Waters of Marah
Selected Prose 1973-1995

The Waters of Marah

David Miller

Singing Horse Press

2003

ISBN 0-935162-25-9

Published by Singing Horse Press
        P. O. Box 40034
        Philadelphia   PA   19106
        215-844-7678
        singinghorse@erols.com

Singing Horse Press titles are distributed by Small Press Distribution, 510-524-1668, or www.spdbooks.org.

 This publication was funded, in part, by a grant from the Pennsylvania Council on the Arts, a state agency funded by the Commonwealth of Pennsylvania and the National Endowment for the Arts.

Acknowledgements and Notes

These writings have appeared in the following books: *The Book of the Spoonmaker* (Cloud, Newcastle upon Tyne, UK), *Dark Ground* (Wild Honey Press, Bray, Co. Wicklow, Ireland), *Elegy* (Oasis Books, London), *Losing to Compassion* (Origin Press, Kyoto, Japan), *Messages* (Torque Press, Southampton, UK), *Pictures of Mercy* (Stride Publications, Exeter, UK), *South London Mix* (Gaberbocchus Press, London), *Stromata* (Burning Deck Press, Providence), *Tesserae* (Stride Publications), and *True Points* (Spectacular Diseases Press, Peterborough, UK). My thanks are due to the respective publishers, Michael Thorp, Randolph Healy, Ian Robinson, Cid Corman, Tim Woods and Peter Middleton, Rupert Loydell, the late Stefan and Franciszka Themerson, Keith and Rosmarie Waldrop, and Paul Green.

I would also like to thank the editors of the magazines and anthologies, too many to name here, where these pieces originally appeared, in part or in whole.

Special thanks are due to Gil Ott for making this present collection possible.

In the same spirit of acknowledging one's debts, I would also like to mention the sources of the brief quotations found in some of these texts, and at the same time gloss one or two things that might otherwise cause difficulties. (A few sources elude me, unfortunately.)

'South London Mix':
Godfrey Miller and Roy de Maistre: Australian painters, both much admired (Miller especially). *She traps drops of liquid…*: this sentence was excerpted from a description of Liliane Lijn's early sculptures, but I am unsure of the source. *And then I had to look at it…*: Kenneth Martin, quoted in an exhibition catalogue about his fountain sculpture for the Brixton Day College.

'Portals':
Parinirvana: this refers to the Buddha's entrance into Final Enlightenment, involving death at the earthly level. The image of the recumbent Buddha's passage into *parinirvana* is an extremely common feature of Buddhist iconography. Fayum: the reference is to the Fayum portraits, i.e. mummy portraits from Greco-Roman Egypt, dating from the 1st to the 4th centuries A.D. (See also 'Aura'.)

'Cells':
…dark stain is how Ruskin characterised the photograph. As with many of the quotations in these texts, I no longer remember the source.

'Threshold':
Soma pneumatikon: spiritual body.

'Bagatelles':
So much have I spoken…: these lines are adapted from a Robert Desnos poem. *…the hecatombs of the concentration camps*: Paul Ricoeur.

'At the Heart of the Thicket':
This text incorporates a passage freely adapted from Eunapius' *The Lives of the Philosophers* and an oracle attributed to Maximilla (collected in Ronald E. Heine's *The Montanist Oracles and Testimonia*, Mercer University Press, 1989).

'Dark Ground':
The quotation from Tertullian is derived from 'On the Resurrection of the Flesh' (*The Writings of Tertullian*, Vol. 2, tr. Peter Holmes, T. & T. Clark, 1870).

'For Patty Waters':
This piece includes some phrases derived from the writings of Madame Guyon.

'Moments':
When a line is cut into many parts…: D.T. Suzuki.

'Stromata':
I quote a few lines from my own poem-sequence, 'Appearance & Event' (*Appearance & Event*, Hawk Press, 1977; revised edition, paradigm press, 1997, incorporated in: *Collected Poems*, University of Salzburg Press, 1997). Izutsu: the writer Toshihiko Izutsu.

'Tesserae':
Fra Angelico's painting is referred to as *The Last Judgement and Paradise* by Ruskin, but is usually referred to as *The Last Judgement*.

Only minor revisions have been made to the texts – including the earliest piece, 'South London Mix' (1973).

One final note: I feel that my writings tend to resist genre classifications. I am a poet, a poet writing in prose (although not exclusively), a prose writer, or simply a writer… as you will. But for those who insist on genre classification, I would venture that the writings in this book are poems in prose, apart from 'Tesserae', which is fiction (or if you like, poetic fiction). I have not included any of my critical writings in this collection.

To the memory of Florence Miller

CONTENTS

"And when they came to Marah, they could not drink of the waters of Marah, for they were bitter: therefore the name of it was called Marah."

Exodus, 15:23

SOUTH LONDON MIX

(for Lawrence Fixel)

1.

At the corner of a church entranceway, a girl sleeps against a wall, in a squatting position, with her legs drawn up and her arms around them, head down on her knees. She is lightly dressed, with cotton T-shirt and frayed blue jeans. Her feet are bare, and brown with mud.

It comes on to rain.

.

There are rooms,
rooms leading to further rooms,
joined together
like an endless road.
You could lose yourself
in these interiors....

I sit with a woman
in a room at night.
We talk
about poetry. As the night progresses
the room darkens about us,
the air cools. Inside:
there are windows and pianos.
Outside: distances manifest themselves
in roads like black tape
interrupted by the occurrence of ponds.

.

I am haunted by the absence of meetings. —Meetings made impossible by deaths — such as those of Godfrey Miller and Roy de Maistre. Or the cessation of meetings, either by ruptured friendship, by the intervention of distance, or again by death. There are interiors I will never sit in, and interiors I will never know again.

.

Aeolian harp, or chimes of some sort (as we had in the room I first slept in, for a few weeks, in South London), that the wind sounds when a window is open.

Imagine the exterior of a house as being sensitive as someone's skin.

The "outside" penetrates what's "inside", if not physically, then in one's sense of a human environment.

What I am saying is obvious. *And* essential.

.

There were white patches left primed but unpainted on the blue ceiling, and when the door was ajar, if you were passing or about to go in, you often got the illusion of a room with the sky as its ceiling.

.

The stain-shapes, ochre, at the bottom of the porcelain sink, sometimes remind me of lovely moths, or rather, the imprint of a moth's life upon another, inorganic presence (as upon celluloid; think of Brakhage's *Mothlight*: though that was not really a film I much liked).

.

The clothes, drying (hopefully),

have become anonymous
white shapes
in the dark yard below.
Not thinking of insects,
earlier I drained boiling water
there from my food.
The clothes, full of dampness
and themselves, have
as their habitation the cold air.
I have temporarily lost them to the air,
to the condition of stones.

.

It used to lie in the center of the garden, a long ochre-orange rectangle bordered neatly by the green of the grass and weeds. She's moved it since. Part of it's draped over the marble-white stone we sit on, near the top of the garden, and it's to one side also (the left), a small fern falls across it.

.

Clothes-lines describe and define a certain type of space in much the same way as a naked body and its particular movements do.

.

I dream your name, you are there, you are not there, the polished teak quietly snows.

.

He took us briefly into a room where another young man (a friend of his), his sister and an older woman sat together at a table. There were not any introductions. The older woman was a redhead with a face as clear-cut as a Modigliani carving, and quite beautiful; I saw her with a clarity in place of the vagueness of perception that shyness usually gives me in strange places. She laughed and said hello, and then he and I turned and went out of the room again, into another (smaller) room.

·

You get up in the early hours woken by a need, then you wash in the dark, in the water-light.

The woman stands in the foreground, straight, head high, but as if she's about to move. *She traps drops of liquid under the clear perspex face of a turntable.*

The others seem less important somehow. She's off-center, to the left, and there's another to the side of her, but partly behind her, you hardly see him.

To the left, in the far corner, another woman bends forward, the weight of her body pressing towards the floor. To the right and further back are two men, one half-lying, half-risen, the other on his haunches, but with his head pointing downwards.

It's too early, you go back to bed.

·

String unwound from her mouth. Or clouds. Floating out.

Drinking. Cups. Blue smoke.

And earth; and light:

·

Brief flash of sunlight across the eyes, bringing one into a different (almost non-visual) space for a second or two, before seeing oneself reflected in the glass of the door.

There the suddenly Suddenly floor, walls, door.

in room brightness. red yellow white There.

.

.

Semi-opaque glass: an area divided with vertical lines. Muted colors of the gray doorstep, the entrance-path, the street, the sky: horizontal whites, browns, greens, blues, all muted. Water.

.

Kitchen door open
to the possibility of rain.
Walking out into the garden,
the house open to this possibility,
I think of concepts, abstract
paintings, soundings of a pond.
I think of death. The luminous
edge of life/death – the oblique –
appears more readily, at times,
at times of rain. The house
takes on other colors.

……………

Reprieve: sun shining, yet cool.
Furniture showroom in Clapham:
uninviting, canned, cold for a cold mind,
pathetic

luxury. My aunt's house, showrooms
from thirty years ago. To walk into it
is to walk into a house out of time, out of touch.

.

A packet of stone-ground wholemeal biscuits, fawn color, circular with indented edges, piled on top of each other into a column, protected and topped by a sheath of cellophane. It sits on the ledge, above the paraffin-heater, and in front of the Italian postcards (the angelic "little loves" of Rimini Cathedral, and the gold, red and white altar of St. Tripun Cathedral), amidst bottles, toiletry (soap and so forth), but in a space of its own, separate. It looks like a stand for a Brancusi sculpture. It is dwindling fast: the biscuits taste good.

.

The task is not even to get a sense of mystery into commonplace things again. I think the job is to reassert the value (and value is not mysterious exactly, *nor* magical, but intangible), of ordinary things. And in doing so, find the place where tangible and intangible meet, and concrete and abstract do likewise.

Again, about simple things: someone once said that a certain line in a poem of mine, 'Briar-Cup', was very beautiful. The line was: *Birds flew over the river.*

.

The wind moves the door a little. It opens onto the lower staircase, leading to the entranceway. The lock of the door is a square of worn black interrupted by rust-marks; the handle is of brown wood, blackened at the top, and with a few specks of white paint. The door was once, I guess, painted white or light gray, but this has been sandpapered down to a milky haze, irregular, over the pale brown wood. I listen to music (Jobim). I want to say something about attention.

.

"Turn quickly on to a floured board, knead lightly for a second only, and then turn into a greased loaf tin. Bake in a brisk oven for three-quarters of an hour."

I hear that the bread which looks at him / heals the hanged man, / the bread baked for him by his wife…. (Paul Celan)

.

The table: a grace. Though I'm not sure what it is to you, who have people here, family and friends, visitors, at table several days a week, maybe more than once a day, to cooked meals. For me it's something out of the ordinary. And the talk: *so.*

.

The easy thing: friends
care for nothing that has to be
ripped from the other, the hard
answer, the demand
that truth be the hawk's truth.
Not the "long haul", and not the flash
of awakening, the rise of ecstasy:
but / a shared and gradual
intimacy.

2.

Guest. Was. Like. Ladybug. He. Garden. Would. Ground. He would. Gently. Place. A. Like. Leaf. Lived. Pond. Whose. Names. Man. Names. Carefully. And. Played. Friends. With. Children. Us.

I. The invitation was. Shy. Wore. To. Gray. Playfully. Buttons. Glass. On. Aging. Quiet. This man.

Was. Game. One. Inconsequential rules, and. Tea. Talking together for. Brief. Several. Writing. Grass.

21

.

It occurs in certain films, where in domestic scenes there is an isolation of certain moments.

.

My image of tao *is not a continuous road but just many dots.* (Toru Takemitsu)

.

Hands. Cloths. Covers. Tables and beds.

Bowls.

And

This.

And

The fish that.

On.

Lift up from.

Same.

In.

Dots.

Orange, red, purple, green, yellow dots.

Leaves spilling water. Mushrooms; grass.

Arrived. We. Purcell. Making. He. A. Fire. When we. Saying. Next. Which. Hear. Described. Hand. Given. Daughter. That. Told. Conversation. Whole. Wished. Listen. Talk. Who. This. Had. See. Late. Two. At. Christmas. Him.

Friend. Upon. Later. You. Attention. Table. House. It. Go. Kitchen. Looked. And. Early. My. Visit. Area.

3.

suddenly (Ashvaghosha)
:*without beginning* (Fa-tsang)
:*without awareness* (Chen-chieh)

Youre two eyn will sle me sodenly (Chaucer)

.

Heart-bowl. Base and sides red.

We dip stumps into it.

.

Dream on a ridge

.

Between black and white, and color – or rather black and white at the beginning of changing, – or would it be the other way, that the colors were at the penultimate stage of disappearing? – It was neither (or both), the image suggesting tints which never quite became evident, mainly a red washed out to a sharp faintness.

·

Between the switch of my water-heater and my table, six paces away, the needle-pricks of a sea make me focus further than before – further than the eraser behind my typewriter, further than the draped glass a few inches away from that. Between these, there is a pile of photographic negative, six or seven strips of it, whose subjects no longer interest anyone. On a diagonal of two feet away, there is a photograph, and this corresponds to what the sea evokes at this moment – a ghostly sea, because it's not there before me, but with the sharp points of light pricking its skin, pricking the eyes.

The sea evokes a woman, and there's nothing out of the ordinary about that. Evokes a way of standing in a room (which is not mine), of standing in a dress, the dress draping the floor it's so long, a way of having the arms and hands, not down at the sides, but at the waist, the hands clasped in front, and as if to have something but not to have anything, but at rest, and a way of holding the head, up and slightly to the side, the eyes a little nervous.

This space, between the light-switch and the table, corresponds to the space between the strips of negative and the photograph, and this is what I am left with.

·

Water. *And then I had to look at it, really look at it. Look at water.* Movements of it, in air, along surfaces, and over itself. And movements of air on water. Stairway, clear.

Time and perception. And perception like water.

·

Numerals. On a glass ruler. – Underneath, what? – Water, again.

·

This pond, this water… its movements (not *movement*) are lines moving past you, and past, past;

24

derivation

and the motions in this circle which is at night so dark and somehow (paradoxically) still, draw you with them, yet you remain where you are as they stream past, ripples in a pond, and the ducks float further from immediate vision. These movements are constant, various, and probably indeterminate; paradoxically there is a stillness. Lines across smooth skin, moving across it, radiating....

At the bottom of the pond a hundred alarm-clocks rust into decay, waiting for the time when they will burst into water-lilies, or strange night-flowers for the blind.

.

...the piano wandering and reflecting within its own huge solitudes.

.

Running down from the tap onto the basin bottom, the water makes a circle that quivers and metamorphoses.

It makes a hole. Like a hole in the sky; a hole in light; a hole in your shadow, whereby I glimpse the womb-warm dreams. My fingers search for portholes.

.

Cloth against skin;
bone and muscle hold to a grace
and a power.
Comb on dresser; letters; on
the floor a weaving-loom:
colors for cloth,
lines that intersect and
move, move and intersect.

Night. Skin: skin.
Face: face. Eyes:
eyes. Cheek: cheek.

Hair: hair. Shoulder:
shoulder. Teeth:
teeth. Waist: waist.
Breasts: breasts. Hip:
hip. Arms: arms.
Hands: hands. A

casual litany, each thing
answering to itself.

.

A psychotic Indian sculptor I met told me that a piece of soap was like a diamond: it cut.

.

A carbon of this one night, a negative of this one day.

.

Darning needles. Crochet needles. Knitting needles. Boot-maker's needles. Sewing needles. Pine needles.

.

Beneath and through us there is a flowing. Nausea; cliché. Stench: sweat and mess that are attendant.

.

The speech of dead birds troubles me. Their speech is like that of a woman whose life was once shattered, and who begins to grow old. The moons look heavy and durable, but they disappear like soap bubbles at the edge of a street.

.

My present boots are the tough sort, hiking boots that is, and made of leather. Which is rare. I avoid wearing leather, just as I avoid eating meat and fish, but I needed shoes or boots, and a friend gave these to me.

Is there anything else to say? – Only that boots (through walking) link up with stones, and stones link up with holes – ruptures, breaks, entries. But that's perhaps to say too much.

.

In a matter of seconds the green-stemmed, purple-flowered thistle changed in color to a dull speckled bone. It approached the brick which lay almost in the center (in width) and at about a sixth of the length of the garden. I used to regard this brick as an object for measuring distances with. But now it's nearly covered over with the debris of deaths.

.

All through the concert I heard the sound of blood beating as if in the distance, yet amplified greatly.

Suddenly a forest broke through the floor.

.

Waiting-rooms. But often
a park, with prior glimpse of her
at a window arranging flowers
as I walked past. Or a friend's

house, nearby. And the car where we sat
outside her home, one in the morning,
friends insisting that nostalgia demands
its vigils and attendances. Garden
and car: flowers and petrol;
and rooms that lead to other rooms,
waiting that leads again to waiting,
poems that lead to more poems....

.

Each day or night, quiet, the manner and conversation charming and polite, the people kind —

That night after I had found out about the hurt and the bitterness, the betrayals, beneath that talk, that quietness, that charm — I wandered the streets sick with a dull tired anger. The figures on posters were suddenly disquieting, rage-provoking. I thought I was back in Melbourne. I walked along Oxford Street, and then down Bond Street to the Green Park Underground. The hard streetlights ached in the night. I didn't want to let go of that quietness, that kindness, those people. And I was sick with my own desire, my innocence, my own hurt and bitterness.

.

Knots. Tea. Breeze. She. It does. It does exactly, as she would and as she does. The breeze is cool, maybe a little more than you'd like.

Alcohol spilling suddenly, copiously, implausibly, over the photograph. Like the destruction of a world.

Again the Pleiades have come out.

This is a sentence. This is also a sentence. This is not a sentence.

.

Janet said this would be the last day we would know. Of course, we didn't believe her. But sixty-two hours have passed since then, and it's still the same day. No one knows how long it will last. The shopkeepers at Clapham South have not closed all this time. Will anyone die? I read Gordon Bottomley and, walking on Clapham Common, reflect on astrophysics and mycology.

.

She walks with difficulty, crosses your path, shuffling, but with deliberation – asks excuse for "embarrassment", asks (blood spots on her hands, breath rank) for a fare with which to travel – where? Do we get anywhere, or do we continually leave and come back?

My friend spends too much time in consumer meal bars; he needs vegetables badly – has a vitamin deficiency. His instinct plays up, and he snuffles grass, drooling, without any idea why he's doing so.

I am tired of the way decencies keep erasing themselves.

.

Photostat hands. Grain. Stet. The imprint of newspaper on wood. Lines on glass: splinterings, cracks, engravings. Things stay. And things disappear. Edges, margins, horizons. Strips of wood. Meeting- stopping- places. Juttings, hoverings, borders. You ride past. Cuttings. The air. Back. Where there is always a sky. Things that go and things that stay. Edges of memories. Of memoirs. Alphabet. Almost. Mossy. Small shining modes. Lace on wood. Deaths occur also. Fragilities / temporality. Precisely. Counting. And there are wings. There are, then, the two things: numbers that you count, and the old man's voice that soars and rides like a bird in air. When you are in love with these things. In the city there is no space, there is only accumulation and gaps. Space becomes a reality again: elsewhere. Stones give you space: space you. Give stones; upset, you set up stones.

PORTALS

– Any such
thing, you say:
doorway, cup,
mouth or hand,
legend congeals there.
– Can't get over it: I've
lost to compassion,
luminous dark point
against which flail
the night's
white shreds, flick-
erings, drum raps.

.

Recumbent –
hand beside head.
Fire over stone,
bells in wind.

The image: *parinirvana*,
caught by the eye
as the bus moves on.

Later: traffic
streaming past,
I sat a long time
in peace.

.

Arch through arch. A face in stone looks in the direction of each cardinal point upon itself, dreams across the ruins, black and white points, patches and splashes of stone, vegetation, ground and sky.

Seated bronze figure, arm off, impossible scale. Behind its profile: the sky, white.

.

A house for blessing the dead, stone dragons guarding past long grass and broken fence: recurring at intervals through childhood into manhood. I stood on the steps, for the photograph; then walked with mother and sister up the street towards a high roof, sun on sheets of new tin. Crowd, wharf and ocean, as extension.

.

I sat listening to a very long piece of music for piano, sustained in its intense quietude and its articulation of a formal architecture intersecting with randomized accumulations of sounds. (– Alpine bells in wind. As we sat together drinking tea, we discussed his work.   – Some of my music, he said, is written with the notes falling 'as quick as lightning'. *But the other pieces* – I follow a strict program for discovering just how slowly I can pace each sound in relation to its neighboring sound. My music, he continued, provides a means – for the contemplation of the way order and chance interrelate in our lives. It is a symbolic interpretation of that interrelationship. My conventions provide me with a way of achieving this with – perhaps I can say – unselfconsciousness.) After a while I became aware of a woman and her child in the front row; the little girl, a blond-haired child with star-shaped ornaments in her hair and a face expressive of the most fetching sobriety, could bear the long duration of this slow, quiet, uneventful music only by attending to her mother's face, holding her hand, and eventually cradling her head first on the woman's shoulder, then in her lap.

.

       Fayum. Only the eyes
       speak, a window
       lets us in

on no other thing. Death

eats all it may. We
have words to bear,
stories that will be told.

.

Music, he said, gives
the right analogy; modes
of expression

analyzed out
into permutations
of features.

The face, I said, effaces
the orders, greater than addition
in the life of imagination.

.

Perpetuum mobile –
mechanical dream –
violin bowed and plucked
in frantic whimsicality:
token, stain on the air.

.

The hands of the huge bronze statue showed reassurance and bestowal. It was raining out there in the garden, a light delicate rain. I had gone there many times when visiting my friend, and I was there again when I couldn't visit him, as he had died several months before. I wandered through its spaces, looking once more at the flowers, the Japanese stone lanterns and the temple bells which rested on the ground; and at the small fountain and the Chinese bronze flower-vessel with a sculptured dragon writhing around its tall rounded form, the dragon's mouth extended wide.

.

Rain upon black branches. At the door: a woman in a red gown, a child before her on the steps. Diadem. Eyes of the mind. – Yellow leaves falling through the darkening air, falling and falling.

.

We looked out from the portals of the old church – out across the city. Bright, spectral blue lights in the square. Groups of people sitting on the blue steps around the fountain, drinking wine. Yet, it was – quiet. He spoke of his admiration for the Siennese masters – Duccio and Simone Martini – and of his life-long attempt to find that same luminosity of color for himself. – Sitting in his studio, I looked at the painting of the Angel of Annunciation, tall robed figure with his head bowed slightly, and a forearm raised, with fingers extended in the making of a sign. The Virgin was outside the space of the painting, the Angel standing at the extreme right, facing out of the edge of the picture. Behind him, in warm, sonorous colors, fruit and a glass stood on a table; behind them, a window looked out onto a serene landscape of hills and trees.

CELLS

Where movement's arrested, an apparition is loosed upon discomforted senses. (I look closer, then closer again, magnifying, brooding.) Snow-visage; snow-hand, reaching out.

.

(Niobe) wept herself to stone.

.

In a photograph – *dark stain* – of a group of strangers, I am struck and held by one face: a resemblance that leaves me stricken.

This young girl (posed with her schoolfellows) fuses with another person, so that I can now see that other as she must have been, years before I first met her.

.

The narrow streets of deep-rutted paving stones, with fountains at the intersections, lead me to this small garden, where she stands, still and solitary. In the night.

.

A contrast of purple flowers and deep green foliage, in sharp light, had drawn my eye. Walking back the same way, night had negated it – permitting a ghostly after-image to remain. The time between: an interregnum.

.

Moved: grasped: shaken: struck: taken up: taken over: flooded: broken apart.

.

Memory: stand again
at her window and see
a sparrow

searching the ground.
Reverse
the positions: I look in

on a bird perched
among decanters,
dishes with pabulum,

everything soaked
in the colors
of an opaque

privacy.
Pompeian
interior. O

where else
to be buried
in ash.

AURA

He was unconscious when they pulled him from the car's wreckage; weeks then went by, with his mother keeping a vigil each day in the hospital.

It was so long a time to be perfectly enclosed within helplessness. But I wake thinking of the body wasted to a skeleton, the wet earth in a hand's grasp before release; and the circle's shaken into flames.

.

The surface of the table, black in darkness, retains deep in its fibers gleams of earring and necklace.

.

Walking in the British Museum, we passed a number of Fayum portraits. She commented that she had made pencil studies of these pictures of the dead from Roman Egypt – which I find more moving than almost all other human images. Later, seated in a café, she asked: Shall I draw your portrait? – No, I replied; I'd rather you didn't.

.

The colors, mixed with the heated bees-wax, form a likeness. Greek lettering, white, spells a name, and the word "farewell".

Those eyes given definition by death look on as if no death could end their seeing.

.

Enduring as faith not as evidence: a fan of yellow, green and blue light framing a head against a white wall.

.

Should I say, *I knew you by your gaze* — I would mean that what endures is the way you arrest and sustain whatever's gathered in your vision. But there is one whose gaze shocks me, and draws love.

A face that reveals more than I'm accustomed to in a person's features. And not in any simple sense; for I cannot say what exactly is being revealed. I am taken into it as if moving along a dizzying projection that I sense as endless.

And if compassion is a visible part of it, so too is pain.

.

Striae, that cut an ambience.

The unspoken penetrates into the table where we sit, in a lambent space where what's loved in the human gaze is irreducible, intractable.

.

In conversation I'd made use of the term *personhood*, culled from the writings of the theologian Heinrich Ott on the spiritual dimensions of personal being. Someone commented, with good-natured mockery, that she liked the term because it made her think of a little man with an umbrella over him.

.

Quavering in the air or the mind: voice composing flame. Cantillation.

He turned at the door. Emptied out his case: the dark green sleeping bag, pullovers, socks, the small pile of jazz records. I saw him, by underground and bus, to the airport, and we parted. As I turned to go back the same way, I realized he was dead.

.

I wake in the dark, amongst the surfaces of things; with the gaze of human eyes impressed through layers of forgetfulness.

THRESHOLD

- If I died, and then reappeared, would you believe it was me? she asked.

- How could that happen? I replied.

- If my body was recreated, and I appeared here again, would you see it was me?

- Could that happen? I asked, turning towards the window, and realizing as I did that it was pouring down outside, yet the sound of the rain against the windowpanes and down in the street had until then made no entry into my consciousness.

.

A kinetically whitened field of vision, street – hail on road and footpath, car-roofs and house-roofs. A doorway sheltered us.

A threshold beckoned to us.

.

– To sit quite still
in the movement first into the dark,
then intense light:
eyes fixed ahead; long
straight hair, pulled back
off the forehead
of the girl's face.

Stopped and drawn forth.

.

And the *soma pneumatikon* would have eyes that would not be yours – and yet be yours; just as the eyes that would recognize them would no longer be identical to those you knew on streets and in rooms and cafés, and yet you would know them as the same.

THE IMAGE

A painter once spoke of how he had tried many times to make an image of the human scream, cry of terror, pain, horror. – And I have always wished, he said, to paint, also, the human smile. It was a wish that remained apart from any known attempt; let alone realization.

.

I imagine you standing on worn steps of stone, with your thin, child's legs; your eager smile; and your gaze that gives back the ineluctable. And the image is terrible to love's eyes – all ruin is spelt to these eyes; each moment, the ruin faced.

.

Streetlamps at the margins, through the central field of obscurity you would move, into the dark. In my room, a lamp's thrust of illumination deforms the outline of its globe. I scrape or rub at the image before me, bringing gray, silver or white from blackness

BAGATELLES

(for Howard Gold)

I picked up the book; on its cover, there were characters in black ink over a gray wash, which I couldn't read. I put it down again and walked along the narrow dark passage until I came out into the blinding rain. – One evening we had been walking together by a canal near where my friend at that time lived, and I found myself thinking of the following fable: In the beginning, the gods placed in a circumscribed area all those spirits who wished to do nothing but continue deceiving each other, hurting each other, acting out all the petty spectacles of egoism which had sustained their interest during their lives on earth: this was hell. But the almost unlimited possibilities of inflicting injury on each other – in the absence of mortality – led the spirits to perform the most gross indignities and savageries upon their fellows and, in their rage for cruelty, themselves. Hell degenerated into a place of perpetual torment and madness, in which its denizens took turns at the roles of dominator and dominated, possessor and possessed, torturer and tortured.

.

So much have I spoken
of you, walked so much,
devoting myself
to your shadow,
that you have gone.
And after everything,
perhaps there remains for me
to be only a shadow
among shadows;
less real
than the shadow that moves
with joy
over the sundial of your days.

(- Voice: which travels along a deathly route, through *the hecatombs of the concentration camps*, ways of manifest evil; bringing words beyond death.)

In dream the figure turned, ran back into the burning house, the sound abruptly cut. – She drank too much, the psychiatrist had said, she was sexually unstable, and she was suicidal; and *this* pathological woman was the most important person in his life. (Saying it in contempt.) – Why shouldn't she have been? I'd replied mildly. And dreamed: felt terror, as I accompanied a huge brown rabbit who stood upright, clothed to the neck with a body-length brown garment. His name was Hunter Rabbit. He kept on shooting people down as we passed them on our way (why was I with him?), taking a snub-nosed gun from a pocket in his clothing. – *Why* are you doing this, for God's sake? I said. – Nuts, he said; those guys had it coming. Back at my place, I took down a book on the painter Bosch, to check out a suspicion that I harbored, while Hunter Rabbit drank his whisky-sour. Sure enough, there he was, except that in the painting he carried a pole from which a naked human body hung suspended by the ankles. – Sure, he said, looking over my shoulder, Jerry the Painter; yeah, I knew Jerry the Painter.

The motorcycle skidded and went over on the dark rainy street, with the rider's leg caught under it. She lay there, her body arched and helpless with shock or pain. – Bombs rip up the streets, rip cars apart and the bodies of people within those cars and on the pavement and road. She tells me this, and the streets and the night take on strange colors, those of another city, another country, fluorescent reds, blues, yellows and greens blurred in the reflection of wet streets, and washed-out pastel colors. A chorus crosses the water: threnody.

DOOR OF PARADISE

A shattered color-slide (steeple against blue of sky, clusters of dwellings, trees). It lies on the circular tabletop among numerous photographs in which one face remains constant – he had sought for an image of her, and found many.

When she was a child he told her stories. Now he's forced to listen to stories about her. – She walks in a trance, he thought, among those who will use her, and then wake her, for their pleasure, to cruelty and indifference.

.

All the doorways we passed through together formed a sequence, enduring over several years – doorways private and public; doorways repeated again and again, and doorways never passed through on a second occasion. And within that long sequence, gaps, marking diverse separations. For she would stop seeing me, caught up at first in parental objections; later, when she had broken with her family, in the fluctuations of her own perplexity.

.

Night: a wall appeared; uprooted and trodden ferns.

And it is proper to have pity for God: so I have heard; so I believe.

.

A line of treetops caught at him. Poverty; urgency. Where the branches end in a final crown of foliage, bloodshed's diminished by each glimmer of light. He is shaken; and these poor trees, that also possess nothing, cry out as what he sees.

.

In a dream, I was with him at a small fairground within sight of the sea. He had shown me a letter:

> I remember that day in Florence when we stood gazing at the gilded bronze doors of the Baptistery; at the Door of Paradise especially, for its splendor. What did all those Biblical stories, each held in an image, hold for me? – Oh father! It's *not* a door – it's a solid wall of gold!

It made me angry. – It's not hers, I said. He was shocked; he didn't believe me.– Damn you, I said; it's not even her handwriting – is it? But he only looked away, so that he faced the sea.

.

A childhood memory: metal trees surrounded by sand. – A *dream?* someone may ask. Tell them nothing, don't elaborate or explain; your hand, the wrist bandaged, brushing back your long hair the wind continually disturbs.

Or else tell them there's still the choice of refuge; or a consuming fire out of the bramble.

LEGEND

The yacht (he said) had twelve drunken poets on board, and when they sighted land they all dove into the sea to swim the rest of the way, and had to be pulled out again.

.

Lines are drawn across or down, or up to lift gaze and smile: as yours are lifted now in the wet and darkened street.

I think of the painter Jay DeFeo, standing full frontal and naked to the waist in the middle of the eyes she'd drawn huge in pencil line.

Do you also stand within the image; is there a story to tell? The affective lines descend and ascend, from your eyes to your pudenda and to your eyes.

.

– And your writing's at an impasse, too! the woman flung at him, at the end of a series of accusations. They sat together in an area bruised to the extent where friendship loses its purchase.

Some months later, he had a dream in which he traced the whereabouts of a singer he'd long admired on the evidence of a few recorded songs of almost thirty years ago. He'd feared a story of alcoholism or drug addiction to account for those years; but when she and her grown son met him at the station and drove him to their house, he found he couldn't believe the supposition to be true of her. – Why, he eventually asked, did you only record those two albums? – I've made other recordings, she told him; it's just that you haven't heard them.

.

Formless yet complete. One register's juxtaposed with another; there are erasures and connecting lines; marginalia.

young woman
in front of me
nothing speaking
between us
like the distance speaks
rows of trees
mist and rain

…form dissolved into feeling.

.

We were remembering events from the past, which had happened in a distant country where we'd both lived. In my late adolescence (I said) I would sometimes catch sight of a young filmmaker who resided in the same house as one of my friends. He was praised for a film that combined animation with live footage, occult symbols with shots of a young woman naked on his bed. One evening I entered the hallway of the house as he was shouting at this same woman, telling her to get out, that he'd finished with her; he was on the landing, and she stood on the stairs below. Her look of pain spreading through disbelief as ink through water caught me; it still catches me — while his film remains as a mere schema.

.

— The heart's affection is enmeshed in vicissitude.

— What's most real is that which we never know, yet there — mid-point, invisible — constancy comes to find itself.

Inscribe these lines beneath a portrait, in which the eyes' impress and the mouth's disposition evoke a perpetual vigil.

AT THE HEART OF THE THICKET

On the walls there are many images. In order to be here, they floated across the water, never getting wet. They *speak by themselves* to visitors.

.

The spirit is good *but the flesh is weak*, my mother wrote to me, *isn't that the saying.*

.

– Why don't you ever talk to people? Why sit by yourself like this each day, in the same tiny arbor?

– Why do you keep watching me?

I overheard two art-school students talking nearby; one said: I went up to that girl in the dirty white dress over there, and she *smelt*. She –

But I closed my ears to what else they had to say. (I'd seen both students walking in the cloisters and at tea in the refectory, parading their clothes spotted and streaked with oil paint.)

A sparrow inspected the grass for leavings, near the exposed, ophidian tree-roots.

.

The woman speaks of her friend, an aging, married man, priest-like in manner and belief, who waited at a college party, so out of the usual, for his young student; and danced with her, a slow dance with glissades, creating a passage through all the people surrounding them.

.

Through the windows of the airplane, the mountains emerge from clouds – monstrous and beautiful in their enormity, their formations; conjuring fear much as a person's presence may bring fear. But with a person, the impress of that fear can be especially deep when he or she is someone you love.

.

At the other end of the park, a dumbshow lecturer stands in the midst of a group of students sitting on the ground. I can only see his gestures, I hear nothing at all: *does* he, in fact, say anything? The figures are small in the distance. There is nothing but two long expanses of grass, separated by a path of stones and earth, between them and where I sit; above us, there is the sky, which darkens.

.

A small group of teenagers, two boys and two girls, lounge around the entrance to the station. As I walk past and look their way, one of them – a tall, strong-looking black youth – grabs the girl beside him by the throat, forcing her against the wall. She catches my eye, and laughs.

.

—You collected the bones and skulls of men whom the law courts had put to death, thinking you were the better for defiling yourselves at their graves. 'Martyrs' you called the dead men, and 'ministers', and 'ambassadors' from the gods to carry men's prayers.

.

Waiting at the entrance of the passage for the truck to drive past, they didn't quite face each other yet neither did they quite turn away; leaves and rain blowing at their faces. Later, they would come to exchange words and gazes.

Wind in the branches of heavy foliage; thoughts struggling with contrary thoughts. Liquid begins to form in the air; then to fall; and, where it has fallen, to soak in or flow off; and, even if colorless, to stain.

She appeared to him in a dream, and said: *I am pursued like a wolf from the sheep. I am not a wolf. I am word, and spirit, and power.*

.

Blue crystal. At the center of the thicket.

.

A house that you reach by a series of narrow lanes past the seafront. Inside, a door opens upon weeping, bleeding, speaking, in their variety of colors.

DARK GROUND

(for Brian Louis Pearce)

The other people there wanted to talk about art; he didn't.

There was a glint of hysteria in his eyes. He said: It was a vast secret society, calling itself the Agapé. Its leaders authored the Christian Gospels, and circulated them for their own worldly ends. They assassinated those whose power they coveted. Montanus wanted to reform the Agapé; he was condemned at Rome, and committed suicide….

.

A woman and a man sit down on a bench by a pond – to talk, earnestly. No sooner have they come to the point of their conversation, than two children commence tricycling around the bench; then a young man asks to have his picture taken. (She smiles, and photographs him.) Finally, another woman sits down beside them. So they leave, continuing their talk as they wander through the park…. She says: We should have met then; by which she means, nearly two decades before – when things would have been possible.

.

– I keep looking at my notes, but not doing anything with them, I said.

He said, Why don't you burn them, and start from nothing?

– Good God, no! I said.

I watched the pebbles plunging into gelatinous water, its color a pale olive-green.

.

Whatever you may chance upon, has already existed, Tertullian wrote; *whatever you have lost, returns again without fail. Nothing perishes but with a view to salvation. The whole, therefore, of this revolving order of things bears witness to the resurrection of the dead.*

Theology informs us in excess, where epigraphy instructs us in too little.

Heads emerge from dystopian holes in the ground.

.

– The naked bulb doesn't emit any light; but across the room, light comes from another bulb hidden beneath a shade....

I felt the necessity for some other rede, equal to the pressure of ineluctable loss.

.

A shepherd and his son witnessed my friend excavating in a remote area, and pitied him and his fellow archaeologists for the penance God had imposed on them. This friend dreamt that he alighted from a bus at the same stop as a young woman playing disjointed phrases on a harmonica – phrases that became more and more frenzied. A short time later he saw her again, as she plunged down from a high building; and her body lay bleeding and lifeless on the ground.

.

Someone is poised at the door, divided by thoughts of going in and of staying where he is. Willful hero, he bears an engraved bracelet to remind him of lions that were slain. But I think of the procession of poor, variegated beasts, *bleached, gilded, or empurpled.*

– All my fear rises up; and it is not for him, but for you. Don't linger in this place, dear.

.

A slow accretion of memories; a darkening expanse of water. The darkening ground.

.

Remembering… her face, her movements, her words that pull the music slowly after them; and the music is as modest and penetrating as a Dowland ayre or a Machaut ballade. Remembering, too, how I followed her up the stairs to a lighted room, where on a table the blue flower grew in dirt.

> her voice entering
> the room's space
> eases anguish and
> with that ease
> ipseity's ruptured
> through the break
> I can attend the words
> long-distance as they
> glisten in darkness
> forming an envelope lost
> like an inset

.

On the notebook's cover a girl stands in a ballet-costume, her face covered in white make-up. Her hands gesture to the sky, an arc indicating lost and soteriological spaces. A secret society calling itself by love's name? I keep thinking of the woman whose ecstatic utterances were nothing the churchman could challenge with argument, leading him to resort to a third type of utterance: exorcism. The woman's followers stopped him from completing the act; yet he had won, all the same. A ring was unknowingly dropped in the dark. Beneath the night, the ground's caked and bleached.

.

Sitting down on the stone, you speak the fragments enclosed as dark within dark.

FOR PATTY WATERS

We were coming down from the top of First Mesa, after visiting an old Hopi woman who lived there; we could hear the singing clearly, even if nothing of the ceremony was visible to us. We'd known from the signs along the road that we weren't allowed to see the sacred dancing, but had decided to go, regardless, to the woman's village. A little girl came up to us and said very politely: Excuse me, non-Indians aren't allowed here during the Kachina Dance; then she skipped past us down the dirt track.

…remember
a child's variation
upon trance

there are souls
it was said
whose faults are as if written

on paper in a dream
the yellow-haired girl and I
stroll by the water's edge

there's a small wound
at her wrist
she mimics the geese's cries

as we walk in their midst
and they lift their wings
to slap against the cold air

there are souls
whose faults are as if written
on sand for the wind

While we were driving through the desert, away from First Mesa, I began to talk about a singer I'd long admired, whose work had been severely marginalized; indeed, it was all-but-forgotten.

Spare, reticent, tender melody was certainly present in her singing, but it would give way to an athematic exploration of sounds that couldn't always be plotted within conventional pitch-notation — and these often seemed extended from such as sighs, moans, screams, cries, shouts. Wistful, passionate, sad, anguished, joyful, serenely resigned, or enraptured. A voice that sometimes appeared to ride on the merest breath, could assume an intensity that evoked a fierce wind. Visited, ecstatically; as part of a *serious game*, a *sober inebriation*. For her distinction was also in the way that her singing took on all the colors of a devotion that passes through the stations of self-abandonment.

Suddenness, transverse.

MESSAGES

The corona in this dark is your being's (mouth pressed tenderly upon mouth). Sending a kiss, I duplicate the sign of unlettered identity.

.

The shapes of interpretation rise up at the borderline between stasis and flux. I trace the oppositions and equations, negations and similitudes; my hand does not cease in the labor.

.

In the stops and breaks of her story, the evening concentrates her glances; her young voice edging towards maturation, tells me in clear tones, "I disappeared from all their lives then", *tabula rasa* which the circulating lines of desire trace, and trace over, and over.

.

Daylight hours were spent asphalting the roads and streets. Black ink ideograms filled the rest of the time: reversed to white in the heart's dictation.

.

What is it which we, looking at each other, can only translate, imperfectly, into longing – into words expressive of longing? – Unity; which is not "beyond good and evil", but rather the "beyond" of good and evil – the transcendence implicit, positively, in good – as its fulfillment; and in evil – as its negation.

.

As in a dream: knowledge bleeds into foreknowledge of fresh atrocities; the dead walk back into corrupt skins, telephone their orders of butchery again.

.

— If you've gathered the flames about you and locked the doors, to die with your signs: how bitter the ecstasies then.

— Melodrama isn't extinguished in café small talk — in its so-ordinary semi-darkness; but in the victims' insistent claim to be heard.

So he seemed to say; and so I thought; and we talked around these things, sitting in a café, looking out at the columns of piled stones in the street.

.

Looking out or looking in: the portico and the door and window are flames. Hands gesture in talk, the fingers spread; the voice catches; and the face, given into my life, endures.

MOMENTS

Graph of durations: grid on which we move. Cut each line on the grid down, down to where thought stops. *When a line is cut into many parts, no matter how many the parts, something will be left. One can never cut into the last unit.*

.

"The hare will never conclude the race which is his love – each moment is divided, cut down further, closer to impossibility. He runs and is still." Ah yes; my hand reaches toward you, reaches and will not reach. Yet even in the photograph, how evident that water has already bathed the wound.

.

Perhaps it's that very moment when the child raises her head, with its shock of auburn hair, to look up at the sky; a look that's immediately cancelled by the sun's too-intense brightness.

Or perhaps it's another selection of time, not an afternoon's blue, but a dawn completely red, orange. Cry out in the midst of it.

STROMATA

Book One

Sitting on a coil of rope, he watched the man fall asleep on a map large as a blanket. The map tore with the man's turnings; pieces were blown into the dark waters.

.

– There was a painter who lived in an island hut, painting at night by a dimly lit kerosene-lamp.

– Almost in darkness…

– He didn't look at the paintings in the daytime. And when he saw them exhibited in galleries…

– Under artificial lights…

– …he'd often denounce them as forgeries.

.

Standing at the sea's edge, waiting for the rain to break, I think of that day we walked together along the mudflats by the river.

She sang the melody without any embellishment; her voice "true", drawing the lines of song through the air.

There was a plant fragment (polypody) caught in her hair. – Don't move, I said; just for a moment.

.

– Figures of infinite regress bore me but *not* him.

I caught the sentence and missed its meaning, my attention more on other things: the fire that had been built from planks and branches; the wine being passed around in paper cups; the two little girls wrapped in their blue sleeping-bags, both girls white-faced after a dip in the cold night sea.

.

A man tells his companion of rituals involving fire and binding (knots, webs). The girl is small and thin; in her middle teens. The man's older. They walk over a bridge, down a narrow walkway, then another walkway; it's dark and there's a strong wind, and this entire riverside area appears empty of other people. She says to him, laughing, Is this where you turn into a monster, now? He walks away from her. She shouts, Bastard, fuck you! but the man, already at some distance, in the gloom beyond the streetlamps' reach, doesn't answer. She shouts again, her voice tearing: Is it over, then?

.

Not even the reed-mats' lines, white powder of decayed material; nor the smashed adornments of *the small princess* – fragments of gold decorations belonging to one so young that her death left her unaccompanied, entailing none of the sacrificial killings familiar to the excavators.

A perfected abandonment.

The eye sees stone, and sees nothing. The wall is quite literally a wall, to which the young woman presses her face, her body shaking as she weeps.

.

During a holiday abroad, my friend sent me a postcard about seeing a film at an open-air cinema, *to the accompaniment of jets landing at the nearby airport, and with the underwater photography mostly washed out by poor projection and too much extraneous light.*

He returned; and one evening we stood together and talked, in the small garden at the back of his house, while the darkness settled. He spoke of the long illness and death of a mutual friend of ours: before these events, he said, it had seemed that similarity, even uniformity, had been most important to him — in persons as much as in nature.

.

Dear – ,

It was too quick for a dream, nor was I asleep as I stood there, having closed the door behind me, and about to switch on the lights. For an instant, a girl was crouched in a corner, sobbing…. And when the lights were on, and I saw that the room was empty, a voice, only just audible, kept calling my name. It was as if the pain you'd related of your adolescence, twenty years in the past, suddenly woke in me. Coulisses? Nothing in the room took on such an aspect; there was nothing there by which I could save myself.

.

A man sits in the dark; listening, nostalgically, to a recording of nature sounds. I don't; I think of a friend, a much-admired older poet. I think of when we sat talking in a café near his hotel; and of how later that day I wandered alone through a park, trees uprooted from the storm of two nights before, each thought of his voice breathing calm upon the air around me. The very sound in memory was my refuge.

Book Two

Sitting beneath the almond tree in blossom, I watched a little girl, the delight in her face simple and frank, skipping the rope held by another girl and an old man.

The dark came, and with it the lighting-up of the streetlamps bordering the park.

(Later:) I listen to Chet Baker singing *Imagination* and *My Foolish Heart*, the voice tender in its candor. *Color so fragile…* it seems *as if it could be blown away.*

.

— …and did you know that your painter crossed the Timor Sea on a raft, starved and hallucinating at the end of the voyage, his obituary already printed?

But those and other details about him had been with me for many years; and I'd once written:

> A lone man on a raft
> crosses a Sea. Imaged face
> becomes almost the shape
> of a paper lotus-petal —
>
> we remember the dead with prayer
> and dream, equally those we love
> who will die. Paper lotus-petal:
> flickering lines across its surface.

.

She stretched over the couch where I was sitting, to pick up the glass of wine on the floor. The arch of her back, the small nakedness between blouse and skirt. In the vertigo born of an upsurge of longing, sight momentarily emptied itself out. — Between her writing desk and mine: so many ways of saying. (Sitting together at a table in the flat that belonged to her absent friend, she'd read her poems to me from the characters that appeared on the small dark blue screen. Her voice composed the details of a mimesis *derived*, as Gadamer says, *from the star-dance of the heavens*.) – And if I look up to see threads of snow falling in my room, like the sea that Su Tung-p'o woke to, where his floor had been…?

.

I was working for a time in a late night bookshop, located – curiously – in a seedy garment district. I was there once during a storm, reading and listening to the rain and the long rolls of thunder, when an acquaintance came through the doorway, dripping water onto the floor.

– Beware young women who believe they're in contact with statues, he said. – A gift for delusions, he continued; sitting in that museum day after day, communing with the damn things.

Looking out the window, I remembered:

> …blood soaks into the carpet
> under bare feet

– but not thinking of him. – There was a window in the poem, with two people standing at it.

> …What sea
> have we come to, it strikes
> the smallest thing: *the radiant heart.*

.

You leaf through the book, looking at the way the colors of the letters are displaced, black by red, for pages…. Misery's singular, however many the lives it possesses; and though assigned to marginalia, its images impoverished, powerless – it claims me in you, claims succor: and I am claimed utterly; so that I take place through this dispossession.

.

– I dreamt I took my children's bones from their graves, washed them, fondled and kissed them… and I awoke raving, with the sun.

— But you don't have any children, I said.

— Yet there was something…, he said; something that held me.

(He'd seen my friend waiting at the bus-shelter, in a memory borrowed from a single photograph; whereas I, long familiar, was rendered invisible.

(Sitting in the disused bear-pit, my two companions and I drank to the spirits — we said — of the dead bears. Later, we saw the remains of the old rheumatology clinic, now mere rubble. And following a path isolated in light, came to a mausoleum covered with scratched inscriptions, the angels' faces mutilated.)

.

A friend writes: I'm sitting here, out of the heat, thinking about what you've written regarding the human image. How could one *ever* be able to paint another person, I've asked myself….

Another friend: We lift the groups of bones, with the earth in which they're found, as one mass — which is then encased in a layer of plaster of Paris.

— *Dream folding into waking life and back into dream, and within those folds, the strands of yourself tearing apart.*

.

Dear – ,

If I think of what is most terrible in a life, the life of someone I love, it is almost entirely unsayable. Unless it is a matter of testimony, how can you say it? Let alone write about it: for personal histories are not "usable"; even though they may be drawn upon, if respect and reticence are the keys to a distinction.

My sister wrote to me, Do you still paint? I hope you do, because you are too good to stop. The picture of a girl with red hair you did in pastel is lovely. — Not only had I stopped — I couldn't remember any such picture; nor even working in pastels. But whatever the medium of portrayal,

I can only approach the idea of imaging another human being with something akin to fear....

Yet in what's said and written and shown, there is always this possibility: time itself called to judgment.

.

He pulled the large drawings out from beneath his bed to show me. Color, as well as imagery, had been displaced. But I thought of Izutsu: *Black here is not sheer black. For in its negation of all colors, all colors are positively affirmed.*

This man, the artist, works in daylight; I write in the evenings. I like to think of Rilke, when he was Rodin's secretary, writing at night, the lamp in his window signifying work done in the night; and the young Cocteau seeing that light, but not knowing for many years that it was Rilke who'd occupied the room.

THE BOOK OF THE SPOONMAKER

(for Tony Rudolf)

It's true I have dreams about non-existent books. The spoonmaker – who wasn't merely a spoon-maker, but that's easy to surmise – spoke against defining good in dependence to evil, as its opposite term. – The room, he wrote, is a trap for flares.

.

I opened the door; a young woman was sitting inside the room, writing. She looked up, astonished to see me there. I had no idea who she might be. She and I took stock of the fact that neither of us was an orphan and she wasn't a widow. (Nor indeed had she ever been married.) On the other hand, we were both from a distant country.

.

The paintings and drawings were acknowledged to provide only limited and fragmented documentation of a special history. I would have liked to have thumbtacked the images to the walls and walked round them with her, one by one; for I wanted to hear what each revealed to her. – You persist in writing about art, when you're supposed to be writing about all manner of other things! And your characters – they *always* discuss subjects that real people hardly ever talk about! I dream of being denounced by breakfast waiters in front of several of my friends.

.

From childhood: a fear of running molten metal, or the sudden din of machinery. We threw our drinks at each other, caught up in a drunken hilarity. At one point my friend gestured towards our host and exclaimed: I think this guy's the Devil! The artist began to write around then over his drawings and paintings. He'd taken the young woman round a private view of another artist's work, loudly denouncing every exhibit with splenetic verbal pyrotechnics.

·

I do end up writing about art, in one sense or another, in most of my work. In divergence, it needs to be said. – What else, she asked, did the spoonmaker say? He said he wanted to redefine empathy in the light of the willingness to be shaken, ruptured, self-abnegated in one's engagement with another person. Meaning and art, he said, could be understood in the wake of such a displacement or dispossession.

·

In Franck's oratorio of the Beatitudes, the despairing thinker is included among those who mourn, together with the orphan, the widow and the stranger. The procession of figures was seen as through tinted glass, the colors shifting between one portion of glass and the next. Locutions were summoned and dissolved by grief. We'd taken the steep path that led up the hill to the castle, my friend insisting upon photographing me at various points along the way. When we were coming back down, I was overtaken by a dizzying, sickening impulse to throw myself from the hillside into the sea below.

·

My friend and I went in search of him and found him in bed, lost to a blissful drunken sleep. No amount of talking, shouting, prodding or shoulder-shaking served to rouse him. The door wouldn't open to our tugging and pushing; and the keys I found in a leather jacket by the bed didn't fit the lock. (When my friend returned from searching the rest of the boat, he informed me that it was his own jacket.) Finally, when we were close to giving up, my friend discovered that the door opened by sliding sideways.

———

...*yellow, blood-colored, violet, water-colored, and grayish-black.* Walking on the bridge at midnight, we found ourselves overtaken by shouts and exploding lights and the noise of glass being broken. The young woman's hand on my arm was the single locus of revocation.

·

Avenues of ivy-covered trees between the long rows of gravestones; pebbles placed on the graves, in remembrance. By divergence: the need, the spoonmaker wrote, to be emptied of oneself. In transverse imitation of the divine exemplar. The anagogical is a limit that presupposes supplementary levels, he also wrote.

ELEGY

One evening we wandered one poorly lit street after another, lost in pouring rain. *Kind*, you said, and rightly, of the two young (very young) street-girls who eventually led us, in a small procession, to the main road.

.

Every now and again something's accomplished. (Names; commentaries.)

.

Marginalia to disjunction, as the lettering around the holes in the vellum seemed. (And the veining: brown-black from the brutality.)

.

Hell into heaven: as a light is switched off by a finger's flick. Gaze into the impossible egress.

.

Without hope, I follow the paths that appear and disappear in dream's indistinct weather.

.

Study shifts, transformations while water drips, domestic. Or flows, spills, splashes; gulls above in a cloud-filled sky.

.

A lyric elegy: the trumpet-player improvises on *Here's that Rainy Day*, against plucked double bass; a dialogue emerging from the solitary sounds.

TESSERAE

Recollection

There were only brief intervals during which Charles slept. For the remainder of what seemed an unending night, he was shaken through a sieve of memories.

.

It rained the afternoon of the funeral. A gray afternoon of heavy rain. Standing at the graveside – among the bowed heads and raincoats. An opulence of flowers.

Tables and chairs; plates; bottle and glasses; papers and books. And the white porcelain bowl, set by itself on a shelf. Each thing, squeezed against the surrounding air, seemed to be waiting. The door, open. Night; plant-fragrances.

.

Charles had been filmed in an Underground station, with half-mask and make-up, wearing a brightly decorative gown and red tights. He was one of a group of nine, five women, a young girl, and two other men, dressed and made-up alike. His friend the filmmaker had wanted to show a vision of the Muses in a railway station, so there they'd sat, clinging to the poles alongside the escalator-stairs. It had snowed earlier; even apart from the icy winds that blew down the escalator, the station was especially cold to anyone dressed in such thin apparel. In one of the nearby corridors, a violinist played discordant sounds to the screeching of the escalators; like the jazz clarinetist Leon Rappallo, gone mad, leaning his head against a telegraph pole and playing to the humming of the wires.

Rid of his disguise, Charles assisted with another sequence, in which Mnemosyne – Memory – was seen approaching her own death. Memory was played by an elderly actress, crotchety and self-conscious of her professional status among the amateurs who made up most of the cast. Dressed and hooded in black, her hair and face whitened for contrast, she was required to emerge, isolated against a black background, from a train carriage; and then walk towards the camera until only the black of her costume was visible.

They were supposed to get out of the train after Memory had been filmed walking towards the camera; but even she failed to emerge from the carriage on the first take. The doors closed and the train moved out of the station while they were still on board. They had to wait in a station shelter among curious strangers, Memory stark white and black, until the next train arrived to take them back where they'd come from.

Later, during a break, Charles sat with the cameraman, Stephen, who was also a friend of the filmmaker's. Stephen produced a small flask of cognac from his coat and proffered it to Charles, who thanked him and took a drink. Stephen had a long, slender, aristocratic face, with dark, plentiful hair; his eyes appeared acutely focused, sometimes on the minutiae of their immediate surroundings, at other times on something apart from what was then present… and a weariness occasionally got caught in his gaze.

.

A few streets, gray apartment buildings, cafés and shops, and parks. Friendships; days that Charles spent with Stephen and with Dore. Those few things, which were connected to each other with lines, like pencil lines, scored over and again so that if it were paper the lines had been drawn on, there would be rips in various places — rips edged with shiny graphite.

Night (I)

– Charles, I can't find Stephen. He's been hurt, and now I don't know where he is; no one I've called has seen him.

– Dore, he said, what's happened?

– I know, she said; everyone thinks that he jumped from the bridge and drowned – but I believe he's still alive. Oh, Charles! I found him before, and I *have* to find him again!

– Are you at home? Charles asked, trying to sound calm.

– Yes, I'm at home, Charles.

– I'll be over in half an hour. Please don't leave before I get there.

– All right; I'll wait for you.

.

An alcoholic woman, smoking and looking out into the thickening dark, sat at the bus stop where Charles waited. Others joined her; the drunken friendliness of a hand awkwardly placed against her cheek wasn't rejected; nor was the gentle indifference of her smile abandoned as she let another man take her wrist to see the time.

The odor of oranges.

.

Charles had been to three pubs in the neighborhood before finding Stephen's group. (They had changed their minds about where to go, and Stephen hadn't thought to phone him.) He sat down at their table, next to a young woman who almost immediately excused herself to go and get some water. A few minutes later she was up again for more water. When someone offered to buy a round, she asked for a beer and another glass of water. After she'd consumed her eighth glass,

Charles suggested they change places so that he wouldn't have to get up every time she did.

Then she began talking to him, not with any chagrin at his remark, but in an utterly dispassionate attempt to enlighten him. She was friendly, too, in a very youthful way. She told Charles she'd been in India recently, where she had contracted amoebic dysentery. Until a few days before, she was under observation in a hospital for tropical diseases; feeling fed up with the confinement, she'd discharged herself by the simple expedient of getting dressed and walking out.

Charles waved a hand at the people at their table, and asked her how she came to be with them.
– Paul is my best friend, she said simply. Charles couldn't help wishing she'd given another explanation, for he already liked her.

Someone suggested that they should all go to a restaurant for dinner. A few people begged off because of prior arrangements for the rest of the evening, leaving seven to find their way to a Greek taverna in the center of the city. Charles rode together with the young woman and Stephen, as passengers in one of the two cars.

– Stephen, Charles said from the back seat, I haven't really spoken to you yet. But something else struck him; he turned to the young woman beside him and said: You haven't told me your name.

– Dore, she said.

– Dore's going to be in my next film, Stephen said. She's going to be the Apostle John. I've always *liked* the idea of one of the Twelve Apostles being a woman.

– Why do you keep the company of such people? Charles asked Stephen, as they were about to part at the Underground station.

– Dore? he said, and smiled.

– No, not Dore. You know who I mean.

He shrugged, and then said: I'm going to use *him* in a film, too.

– I'm appalled that you associate with him at all, Charles said.

Stephen made no reply. The matter annoyed Charles; but not, he knew, entirely for his own sake. He tried to think of why Dore should like Paul. He supposed she thought him a humorous young man, in love with enjoyment. But Paul would have enjoyed the unhappiest, most tragic of situations – as long as it was someone else's; he would have reacted to it with a distanced, frigid display of wit. Charles had always known that.

.

Dore was playing a recording of Boyd Raeburn's band, from the late '40s: *Black Night and Fog*, with Dave Allen's voice against woodwinds, double basses and acoustic guitars. She followed it with another Raeburn track, *Eagle Flies*.

They sat together without saying anything, listening to the music. Then:

– Dore, we must talk, Charles said.

She nodded. Charles went to the kitchen, and came back with two glasses of brandy. She was playing *Black Night and Fog* over again, singing to it, for the most part wordlessly, except in the few instances where she recalled the odd phrase.

.

– She thinks she's been killed, Frank said. That she was killed, and walked away from her death. Swam away, at any rate.

– She doesn't think any such thing, said Charles. That's not what Dore believes at all.

– All right, she thinks her body was terribly mutilated, he said, and then miraculously healed. It's the same thing – death and resurrection. Isn't it?

– That's not the story she's told me, Charles said.

– But she *did* tell you that the Stephen she found was someone wounded, his body lacerated and bleeding profusely?

Frank's voice had grown bright with irritation.

– Yes, said Charles.

– And that his tormentors had said to him, "You whore, this is only the beginning" – as he crouched naked before them?

– You're making that part up, Charles said.

– Oh, really? Frank said.

– She'd taken opium; closing her eyes, she saw a series of fluorescent dots, that soon arranged themselves into two cartoon characters: an upright-standing mouse, rather like Jerry of Tom and Jerry, who gestured to her with his gloved digits to follow him, and a sparrow that similarly beckoned with its wing. Together they led her down to the beach; "Wait here", said the sparrow, and the mouse said "Now don't go away." They vanished; and eventually she fell asleep. When she woke up, she searched the streets along the front until she found Stephen.

Frank sighed. A comfortable, smug man, Charles thought him. He said: Are you *so* safeguarded, Frank?

– Why are you evading so much of what's happened with Dore? he said.

– I'm reminded, Charles replied, of a dream I once had. No, don't interrupt; just listen for a minute. My dream was in the form of a newsreel. It concerned some archaeological findings about a barbarian cult-group, notorious for rapine and cruelty. What the archaeologist declared before the news cameras, was that all the bones that had been found were those of male adolescents; and there were ritual objects in the graves that suggested the cult members were dedicated – not to brutality – but to acts of good will. "In fact", he continued, "they might be thought of as forerunners of the Boy Scouts." And at this point in the newsreel, it was announced that the Boy Scout movement had resolved to redeem the reputation of this ancient cult, whose members were, so to speak, their ancestors.

– Do you mean that we fail to see the good in people? That we're misled by reputations and labels?

– No, said Charles.

Occultation

– Dore, Charles said, why don't you go for a walk along the seafront?

It was like saying, "Go away, Dore"; but Charles couldn't avoid it. She looked at him, and at Frank, helplessly; then she walked away on her thin legs – legs that always made Charles think of an undernourished child.

– Why on earth, Charles said, did you have to get Dore to come and tell me?

Frank lifted his gaze to Charles'. He said:

– I've got the paper right here. Do you want to see it?

Charles took the paper from him and read the small item that had been circled with a pencil line. It was headed *Suicide by Drowning*.

– God, he said; eight shitty lines, of an inch and a half column.

.

There had been a series of signs. Stephen was eating lunch in a cafeteria, when a woman walked in, so like Portia that he felt he'd been struck across the face. He happened to glance at a TV set in the far corner of the room, and saw a car wholly enveloped in flames, small in the dark distance of the image. A short time later he found a ring, implausibly, in his yogurt. Rings, resemblances…. These things were part of a banal currency, he knew, yet not any the less authoritative for that.

.

A girl stands small against the immense gate, fence-posts stretching away on either side, the building towering black above her…. In the foreground, white petals are falling on the red roses below. Later – many years past – she stands beside stone steps, leaning on the railings; coat over her arm, a string-bag in one hand, a book in the other. The two large, long windows of the café seem black glass, the café's name spelled out at the top of the right-hand window in bold green letters; closer, the glass is merely dusky, the people inside dimly visible beyond it. She is tall and thin, waif-like, with unkempt hair the color of straw.

— I woke on the beach, she says, when it was dark; I was wet, and cold, and I went to find somewhere warm. I walked for a long time, until I came to a parked car with one of its doors open; and someone inside was crying, softly, with pain. It was the loneliest sound. I went up to the car, and bent over to look in. It was Stephen — but he looked like a hurt child, and there was blood all over the seat. I cried out; and he said: They'll be back — the men who did this to me; please help me!

— He didn't tell me who they were, she continues, or why they'd hurt him. I helped him from the car (I can't drive, and he was too injured to try), and we walked a little way, with me supporting him. But I couldn't do it for long…. So I had to leave him, crouched in a doorway, while I searched for a taxi. When I came back to pick him up, he was gone. I made the taxi-driver go round and round the area, but we never found him. I thought those men must have reached him before I did. But I've kept hoping that someone else might have found him, and cared for him.

The tree's shadow, swaying across the pathway, reached to where they sat together on the warm ground. The lines of the branches and the clustered leaf-shapes composed a web, its design fluctuating with the wind. She looked up from her reading. — What is it? she said.

— Nothing. I was only thinking of a Chinese porcelain dish I saw once — with rust-brown tracery of branches on a white ground.

She was silent, as if waiting for Charles to say something more.

— No, that wasn't *all* I was thinking about, Charles said. I was thinking that I never know how much to believe of what you say.

And immediately, regret and shame caught at him.

Charles found her sitting in the near-dark, a single candle on the table, next to some roses in a glass of water. Neither the candle nor the flowers had been there earlier. He was pained by the folly of their having come to this town, in the hope of finding Stephen. He'd bought oranges and peaches from a fruit-shop, and he put them down on the table. Dore started. There were tears on her cheeks. — Why the candle? Charles said, not quite knowing the reason for asking — except that it was better than saying something about her tears.

— When I was a child, she said, I made candles, I collected them…. And Stephen —

— Yes, said Charles, I know. Stephen was fond of candlelight, wasn't he? He said that there was an immaterial quality to the light, while it seemed palpable at the same time. He felt there was something similar about a film image, and the light within the image.

— What's it for? Charles asked.

— Divination, Collin said. It's a scrying ball. Would you give it to me?

The globe, clear and light, was hung by a doubled thread from the ceiling; it had been a present, but Charles had lost track of the friend who'd given it to him.

— Silvered globes can be used, too. You really didn't know what this was for?

— No, Charles said. You can have it, if you really want it.

Collin had arrived during a downpour. His shoes leaked, and he took them off when he came into the lounge.

— But chance is what really interests me most, he said. Coins, dice, anything of that sort. Ah, you must be Stephen?

Stephen, who'd been in the bathroom when the doorbell rang, stood at the entrance to the lounge. — Yes, he said; and you're Collin — Charles has told me about you.

.

Charles and Stephen stood in front of Turner's *Angel Standing in the Sun*, in the Tate's Clore Gallery. Charles had never seen the painting before; and found it remarkable. The Angel stood within a swirl of dirty light — was *this* the Sun? Charles wondered. A swarm of birds were invoked by the Angel's raised sword — and the birds gathered as if to fly towards them, Stephen and Charles, in the time yet to come, as much as to prey upon the figures in the lower part of the painting. The golden substance that spilled from the figure of the Angel, modulating to yellow in places, was smeared with red, and manifestly fatal. Yet the Angel's gesture at the same time resembled some strange benediction, even if the fleeing humans were not under any sway of blessing.

— Those demoniac birds…, Charles began to say; and then: No, not demoniac. And he said no more.

— I've often thought of including the painting in a film, said Stephen. That's why I wanted to show it to you.

.

Stephen's eyes took in all manner of things, and the thread of his vision drew lines from each to each, drawing them together. Some people behaved as if the persecution of the faithful was the mirror image of the punishment of the damned. Others' eyes encapsulated, in their manner of looking, lust; or hatred; or murder. But there was a "no" that seemed to be projected from Stephen's very receptivity, calmly suffusing his gaze. He had a severe and ethical cast of mind, which oriented his natural and deep capacities for curiosity, and for kindness. That, at least, was how Charles saw him.

.

— My wife and I once took a car-ride to a small island, near enough that we could drive to it in a few hours, with no other redeeming feature (as it turned out when we got there) than the sea. We walked out on the mudflats that cold, windy afternoon, the water a gray-blue color, and no one else to be seen. That memory is a remnant of time in negative, in the same way that you can have a photographic negative. My wife, Portia, left me; but my affections are furthered, like plants that continue to grow, through that image and others of its kind.

— It doesn't sound a particularly happy memory, said Collin.

— Oh, it's *perfect*, Stephen replied. After a pause, he added: Uranian. So's Portia.

.

— Don't forget to give me the scrying ball before I go, said Collin. I don't want to be rude and take it down myself.

— You believe in it? asked Stephen.

— Yes, of course, Collin said, smiling at him. And I keep a sigil of Venus on a chain around my neck. What else do you want to know?

But Collin was thinking, not of the transparent globe nor of the sigil, but of the woman he'd seen with Stephen earlier that day in the café, and of how Stephen had tried to embrace her. Was she Portia? he wondered. Yes; and it shook him that the fury *he* felt beneath the sound of the rain and the wind, and the music (Barraqué's) they were listening to on the CD player, the sexual fury sweeping back and forth behind all that he heard, and that he saw, seemed absent from this young man. – But he remembers, he dreams of her, Collin thought. There are places and times.

.

Collin sat down with his morning coffee, and began looking through the paper. He stopped at the photograph (from a news item of another city) where three men stood on a hydraulic platform behind a stone swan, with lifted wings, on top of the clock tower of the town hall. A flagpole near the bird had been broken off by violent winds.

As monolithic in the totality of its appearance and effect, and fragmented in intimate detail, as the music by Barraqué they had listened to the evening before: so fate (as he called it) seemed to him. He believed in the astral dictates that controlled events, and he believed in chance; and not as opposites, but as one and the same. It was a matter of interpreting the chance occurrence, so that it revealed its true message. – And this – this image? he asked himself, and wondered.

Principles

Charles lived a short distance from one of the colleges of the university; unemployed, he spent a considerable amount of time in the college library, pursuing private studies. If he was there for both the morning and afternoon, he'd eat in the refectory. One lunchtime someone left a photo-copied notice on his table; it advertised a screening of films by postgraduate students. Stephen's *Persephone* was among them.

Persephone, Charles felt, was clearly related to the films of their mutual friend, with whom they'd recently worked – at least, in the way it used Classical mythology for its own cinematic purposes.

Charles went up to Stephen after the screening, and said: Stephen, you make films as if you were a painter.

– I am a painter, he said.

– I didn't mean it as a compliment, Charles said, and immediately regretted his rudeness.

Stephen laughed, however. – Did anything else strike you about the film?

– Yes. I've been in those places, too.

It was the beginning of their friendship.

.

– *For love they have no care*, Stephen said, *none for the widow, none for the orphan, none for the distressed, none for the afflicted*. But, he continued, raising one finger and then pausing for a moment: they're not very wise, either.

– Do you believe in evil spirits? Charles asked.

– I believe, said Stephen, in the existence of the monstrous; in what's worst of us, and which transgresses the bounds of what's rightly human, in its destructiveness; and which, magnified and intensified, we name as devils. Yes, I believe.

– I remember, said Charles, that I once became involved in an argument with a member of some peculiar cult, during which I was gravely informed that illnesses were the result of possession by the spirits of dead people – people who had led immoral lives. But at least she and her fellow believers were committed to something. They had an honest relationship to their own idiocy. Paul haunts his own body, and if others are taken in by him and think he's a real person rather than a ghost – then God help them. Because I believe he's something corrupt that's taken on the semblance of the living, and people are tainted by contact with him.

– There's a tradition that Christ went down to Hades, Stephen said, in the interregnum between His death on the Cross and His resurrection. He descended to preach to the souls there, and save them.

– And I've never known anyone, said Charles, the word "perdition" seemed more nearly meant for, than Paul.

.

– That image of the girl, standing against the gate, the building towering above her…. And the close-up of the white petals falling on the red roses beneath them…. You could never have caught those images in any other medium, not in that way: so that they're actual in their physicality, yet ghostly at the same time.

– Yes, but Charles has a different view of the film.

– Oh?

– They're good images, Charles said; there are many good images in Stephen's film. But it's all too static, too composed, too much like a series of vignettes. He's a painter, and it's a painter's film – that's all I've ever said.

– You say it like there's something wrong with being a painter, Frank said.

– No; I suppose I'm being a purist.

– But all the same, said Stephen; I'm dissatisfied with what's been achieved in the cinema. Perhaps the cinema needs painters. Painting doesn't need anything, because it's already reached its conclusion: there's little left now but to play around with the shards of an exhausted tradition. Filmmakers have done so little with their art – not counting a few exceptions; why shouldn't painters make what they can of it?

Some discussion, then, of how cinema stood in this regard: with considerable conflict, and some agreement.

– I want you to be pulled through a movement of images, and to be brought to a stop, suspended, with a shock. And in that stillness, I want to show a moment when some thing or other appears both strange and perfected – as if part of a resurrection world. Or in the image of a laburnum tree, with its clusters of small yellow verticals, I'd like you to see the earth with the beauty it had at the moment when the wise men adored the Christ child.

– But, Charles said, you could let those moments emerge from the development of the film, the progression of images and words – without resorting to still images....

Charles couldn't *see* them together, Stephen and Frank, although they stood facing each other, Frank beginning to tell Stephen how petty he thought Charles' point: Stephen slim and boyish-looking, Frank overweight and prematurely middle-aged.

Charles looked at the young woman, Dore, who sat by herself in the opposite corner of the room, reading; and thought: she's that child, standing at the gate.

.

In some curious way, Paul admired Stephen, with a giggling enthusiasm that remained blind to who and what Stephen was. He seemed to find Stephen "glamorous" – an artist-hero figure who could be the subject of his "appreciation": which was both naïve and cynical in its blankness.

Stephen had planned to cast Paul as the tormentor of an innocent victim in a film he had in mind, where the victim would pass through those stages of the Passion Guilloré analyzed in his *Conférences spirituelles* in terms of the mockery of a divine fool. (For what else could Christ seem to be, in the ignominious and unworldly role he plays before Herod.) This was, for Stephen, the only legitimate way to deal with someone like Paul: by an act of recognition.

.

– Do you know Holman Hunt's painting, *The Triumph of the Innocents*? Stephen asked. It shows the children slaughtered by King Herod appearing in their resurrection bodies to the Holy Family, during the flight into Egypt.

– Yes, Charles said, the children's bodies are as if sunlit, and everything else is in moonlight. It's a very mechanical solution….

Stephen looked at him askance.

– I mean I'm too aware of the mechanics of it. Isn't it like those spirit photographs that were once so convincing? It doesn't work now….

– It works in the way that collage works, Stephen said. And that's how I want to develop this impossible combination – life and afterlife, vernal reality and resurrection – in a film I'm planning. Ruskin says that Fra Angelico's *Last Judgement and Paradise*, and Orcagna's *Last Judgement*, are *real visions of real things*. That's what I want to show: real visions of real things.

Descent

Stephen was sitting up late one night, working on some notes, when the telephone rang.

The voice, Dore's, said: I'm sorry to ring you at this hour, Stephen; did I wake you?

— No, you didn't wake me. Are you all right?

— I have to see you, Stephen.

.

— One short film and a list of projects that he never got to realize, said Frank; it's an enormous pity.

Neither Charles nor Collin said anything in reply.

— I knew from the start, said Frank. I knew he was a greatly talented man; and I sensed he'd come to grief.

Collin thought of his own suicide attempt, years before, when he was in his middle teens. In the hospital, one of the nurses said to him: We don't often get such nice boys in here. — Go to hell, he'd said.

He felt like saying the same thing to Frank.

— How? asked Charles.

— How? said Frank. What do you mean, "how"?

— How did you know he'd kill himself?

— I sensed that he wouldn't find an outlet for his energies, and that he'd turn against himself.

— You seriously believe that's why Stephen committed suicide? said Charles.

．

Stephen was describing a visit he'd once made to the temple at Delphi; arriving in a rainstorm, he'd waited until the rain cleared to ascend the hillside, only to encounter a fresh burst of heavy rain and descend again; and this became the pattern for the better part of the afternoon.

Charles said: Yes, I was also there, late last year; but at that moment he was distracted by seeing Paul strolling in their direction, on the way to the drinks table. – Chichi young man, thought Charles, with your raddled face. Then, as Paul and his companion passed by, he heard the other man ask, laughing: What was it like, sleeping with Dore?

．

Something about Collin disturbed Charles. – Too handsome, and aware of it, he thought; with his intense dark eyes, his sensual features, and his massed thick black curls of hair. He also remembered waiting for Collin outside a public toilet, only to have Collin emerge with an adolescent he tried to make out as an old acquaintance. – Really? said Charles; and the boy laughed at the pretence, handed Collin a coin, and walked away.

Yet he had to admit that he found Collin charming: sufficiently so, that he had continued to see Collin, at intervals, over the years.

They were sitting in Charles' flat, and Collin remarked upon the unmistakable vocal noises of pigeons, and their less easily identifiable scrabbling, coming from the ceiling. – There's a rectangular hole in the front roof, Charles said, where a tile's gone, above the middle window. – And the noise? said Collin. – Good God, yes, said Charles; it's terrible.

– Do you remember, Collin said, the glass ball that you gave me?

– Yes, it was the first time you and Stephen met.

– Well, I smashed it.

Charles was sitting with his head resting against his hand, the elbow propped on the table; his gaze diffident.

Now he sat up, with his head inclined on the other side; his nervous hands one on top of the other on the table; a small and unhappy smile beginning to emerge in his eyes and taut mouth.

– Why, he said quietly; what was the matter?

– Memories, said Collin; the recent past – Stephen, I mean.

.

Stephen stood in the doorway of the room. He was amused at finding a hotel where the proprietor looked like Mircea Eliade, and it occurred to him to write a letter to Dore, mentioning this fact.

That night he dreamt he was sinking through water, further and further; and then he saw a number of dark, tripartite shapes, the middle part of each knobbed at the top, the outer parts, spread horizontally, beating, flapping, driving the shapes towards him through the water. – Ah, to float like wood, he thought. As the shapes converged upon him, he felt no threat – only a dark comfort, that covered him.

.

Stephen looked at Charles in that arch way he always adopted when he made use of a quotation:

– I know a way, he said, but it isn't easy.

– Have you read *The Testaments of the Twelve Patriarchs, the Sons of Jacob?* he continued. *Love would quicken even the dead, and call back those who are condemned to die.*

Interregnum

Charles woke into stories, with the bells from the nearby tower:

– I want you to run down there and find Charles, and tell him what's happened, Frank said. He drew Dore towards him, so that they stood together, looking down at the promenade.

Walking in a garden, Stephen sees white petals – like snow, fallen upon red blossoms….

.

– What are you reading? Charles asked her.

Dore showed him the book: it was *As I Lay Dying*. – Stephen gave it to me, she said. I like it, but it's a bit odd.

– What were you doing in India? he said.

– I went with a friend. He disappeared….

– Disappeared?

– Well, he got involved with a woman we met in the house where we'd go to smoke opium. One night I went back to the hotel after a walk, and he was gone. I waited around until I was sure he wasn't going to return, then I came home.

– How often have you taken opium?

– Only a few times, Charles. I've taken all sorts of things, but don't worry, I'm not some kind of addict! She laughed – a shy, slightly anxious laugh.

– And now?

– I'm only using poppers, nothing else.

– Poppers?

90

She smiled, and took two small bottles of a clear liquid from the refrigerator; she gave them to Charles to hold.

He handed back the cold bottles, none the wiser.

– Do you drink it? he said after a silence.

– You *sniff* it, she said; it makes you lose your inhibitions. She held out one of the bottles to him again.

.

– There was a semi-demolished building on the way to the café, said Collin, and as I walked past it, I felt that someone was staring at me; I turned, with a start, to see only the remains of a fire – a few pieces of wood, still burning.

– I went into the café, ordered a tea, and seated myself. Then I saw Stephen (although, at the time, I didn't know he was Stephen); he was with a strikingly attractive young woman – her features had a brittle perfection; but behind the perfection, and the distant manner of her gestures and bearing, there was a distinct suggestion of anger. I was seated across from them, a few rows back. Stephen tried to put his arm around the woman; she turned from his embrace, and sat looking away from him. She lit a cigarette, exhaling the smoke through her nostrils. Stephen went on talking (I heard his voice without being able to make out the words), while she remained disdainfully silent. He seemed unable to look anywhere but at her. I saw, quite clearly, that she would be fascinating… to some men.

.

– Are there any photos of Stephen? Dore asked, looking through a stack of prints on Charles' desk.

– No, he said; but Stephen took some of them.

She looked back through the pile, and looked at them longer this time; taking time to sense the eye, the person, behind those images.

It was a neatly arranged garden-park, pleasant and restful, if lacking in any great variety or anything especially vivid.

From where Stephen stood, on the small stone bridge, he could hear the voices of the birds (predominantly shrill, sharp) from the aviary a short distance away.

The water below was a dark green broken by the sky's fluid reflection, and by the geese that floated there.

He looked down, and then closed his eyes.

– Come back, please come back, he said; almost visibly shaking as he said the words.

– Should I wait? he said. *Will* she come back?

His hand unclenched to drop the gold ring into the water below; and he quickly leaned over the railing to watch what then occurred.

Stephen walked back over the bridge, towards the aviary. He saw someone standing there, with a sketchpad in his hand.

Night (II)

She appeared in the doorway of the room, her hair glittering with raindrops. She smiled when she caught sight of Stephen.

They stood together, talking, not bothering about the other people there or what else was happening in the room. Their hostess, already foolishly drunk, stumbled across to them, spilling wine. – Who's this young man? she said to Dore, as she refilled their glasses. – Stephen, Dore said simply.

The woman turned to Stephen and said: Are you Dore's lover?

– No, said Stephen.

Dore playfully slapped him across the arm.

– You're supposed to say "Yes", she said.

    .

They walked that long street bordering the park. At the hill's top Stephen and Charles headed towards the clusters of people, and the cinemas, shops and eating-places, brightly lit beneath the night sky.

    .

– I've changed my mind, said Dore. I don't want to talk with you. Go away, Stephen.

– What does he want from you, Dore?

– I love him, she said.

– And?

– What more should I say? Isn't it enough to tell you I love Paul?

Stephen put his arms around Dore, and gently pressed her against himself. She began to cry then.

– You didn't get me to come over at this time of night just to tell me that you love Paul, did you?

– He wanted me to kill someone – this girl, who'd once rebuffed him. He said it didn't really matter who it was; there wasn't any point to it except that it would bind me to him more fully.

– But you didn't do it, said Stephen, kissing her hair.

– It wasn't possible, she said.

.

– So Paul refused to see her again after that? Charles said.

– Yes; and it's the best thing for Dore – needless to say. She doesn't see it quite that way, unfortunately.

– She's too vulnerable, said Charles.

– Yes, she *is* vulnerable, replied Stephen. But that's partly what makes her beautiful, as well as it being her misfortune. And what about you, Charles?

– What else happened? asked Charles, ignoring Stephen's question.

– Nothing. Except that I slept at her place, on the couch – rather than walk all the way home. During the early hours I was awoken by noises in the kitchen, and when I went to investigate I found Dore with her head in the oven. She was asleep, mind you, and the gas wasn't on. I woke her up and got her back to bed. Did you know she sleepwalks?

– No; she's never mentioned it.

– She acts out things that she's dreaming about. I can't say I like the idea that she dreamt about putting her head in the oven. She told me that she's been known to sit cross-legged on her bed, laughing, with tears running down her cheeks; and she's been asleep the while.

They parted at the entrance to the Underground station: Stephen wandering off to find a bus back to his home, and Charles descending into the station.

Charles bought a ticket, and walked over to the turnstiles. A bunch of tulips lay on top of a turnstile, the red of the flowers and green of the stalks vivid against the silver color of the polished metal. The sight of the flowers sealed his pain. He was immediately in tears. – Seal, he thought; seal of grief.

Spoliation

It was early evening when they arrived at the hotel and booked into their rooms. The hotelkeeper was a small, thin man in his sixties, with a lean, ascetic face and horn-rimmed glasses. Stephen had written to Dore: *He reminds me of Mircea Eliade, the historian of religions; I'm delighted by the idea of Eliade running a cheap seaside hotel to finance his research.*

The man remembered Stephen, when Frank showed him Stephen's photograph. But he said that Stephen had left no forwarding address, nor mentioned any plans, when he moved out five days before.

.

Stephen sat alone on a bench on the promenade, writing in a notebook with an orange cover.

A tiny girl, wrapped throat to ankles in a plaid blanket, stood on the pebbles at the sea's edge, watching the waves break, and feeling the splash of the water on her feet. Old people, mothers with children, and adolescents playing hooky occupied the deck chairs and benches: Stephen felt conspicuous, fitting into none of the dominant groups of daytime idlers. He stopped writing from time to time to observe their comings and goings, or to watch the gulls, sparrows and pigeons that wandered the promenade for scraps.

.

He wanted to put on the lights, but she asked him not to: so they sat together in the candlelight, Dore drinking coffee from a bone-colored cup; both of them too distracted to talk.

Then: – Do you remember the letter he sent me? she said. The last one?

– Yes, of course, said Charles. Would you read it to me?

He wanted to hear her voice speaking Stephen's words. Why, he didn't know. He also sensed that Dore wished to read the letter to him; even though they both remembered very well what it said.

The sky's fluid reflection; the dark green of the water. An aviary stood only a short distance away: so that the predominantly shrill and sharp cries of the birds were clearly audible as Stephen stood on the stone bridge. He looked down, then closed his eyes.

.

– I'm sorry, Stephen said. I thought you were someone I knew: a friend from art school. The man was standing, sketchpad in hand, in front of the cages of exotic birds – the birds which Stephen especially loved. On an impulse, Stephen said: But could I see what you've been drawing? The man handed him the pad without a word; and Stephen saw that he'd turned the birds into various bizarre figures, half-avian, half-human.

.

Charles was strolling in a park near the promenade. He stopped in front of a tiered profusion of flowers; the different colors gaudy, excessive, in combination. He stood there for an uncertain – but long – period of time; not really thinking: rather, his mind awash with fragments of thought and memory.

He turned around and saw, with a shock, that Dore was standing there; tears streaming down her face.

.

– I don't understand why he became so concerned with Christian themes, said Frank. That first film of his… his *only* film: that was something quite different.

Charles looked at him sharply.

– He'd turned away from his original inspiration, Frank concluded.

– Did you know, Charles said, that he was making notes for a film called *The Spoliation* shortly before he disappeared?

·

She continued:

– Please *try to detach yourself from thoughts about Paul. Why do I beg you to do this? Not because he's abandoned you, Dore. Paul is the sort of person who's dominated by an obsessive lusting after "experiences", especially when they're "forbidden"; and this might be mistaken for a longing for knowledge, except that it lacks any sense of discrimination.*

– *Even if he meant well by you (and I don't think he ever has), he could never do anything but harm you.*

– *And think of how he* has *treated you. For this is what I believe: that the pursuit of power over others surrenders us to what is worst of us; and makes us a prey to powers…. We need to abnegate all desire for power and dominion.*

– *I'm sorry if anything I've said seems brutal, Dore. All that I've said has needed saying.*

– *As for myself…. I've gone away, because I need to consider certain things, and it doesn't appear possible to do this except while wholly alone.*

– *And finally, Dore: you have my love, and always will; no matter what happens.*

Stephen

– And the postscript, said Charles.

– Yes, she said; and read it out:

– *A beautiful saying, from Theophilus of Antioch: "Is there not a resurrection for the seeds and the fruits?"*

·

He woke into stories, with the ringing of the bells.

SINGING HORSE PRESS TITLES

Ammiel Alcalay, *the cairo notebooks*. 1993, $9.50
Asa Benveniste, *Invisible Ink*. 1989, $4.00
Julia Blumenreich, *Meeting Tessie*. 1994, $6.00.
Linh Dinh, *Drunkard Boxing*. 1998, $6.00.
Rachel Blau DuPlessis, *Draft X: Letters*. 1990, $6.00.
Norman Fischer, *Success*. 1999, $14.00.
Eli Goldblatt, *Without a Trace*. 2001, $12.50.
Karen Kelley, *Her Angel*. 1992, $7.50.
Kevin Killian & Leslie Scalapino, *Stone Marmalade*. 1996, $9.50.
Kush, *The End Befallen Edgar Allan Poe*. 1982, $2.00.
McCreary, Chris & Jenn, *The Effacements / a doctrine of signatures*. 2002, $12.50.
David Miller, *The Waters of Marah*. 2002, $14,00.
David Miller, *Unity*. 1981, $3.00,
Harryette Mullen, *Muse & Drudge*. 1995, $12.50.
Harryette Mullen, *S*PeRM**K*T*. 1992, $8.00.
Gil Ott, *Pact*. 2002, $14.00.
Heather Thomas, *Practicing Amnesia*. 2000, $12.50.
Rosmarie Waldrop, *Split Infinites*. 1998, $14.00.
Lewis Warsh, *Touch of the Whip*. 2001, $14.00.
Vassilis Zambaras, *Aural*. 1984, $2.00.

All titles may be purchased directly from the publisher. Send check or money order, plus $2.00 for postage and handling, to: **Singing Horse Press,** PO Box 40034, Philadelphia   PA   19106-0034   USA   Phone: (215)844-7678, or email: singinghorse@erols.com.

Bookstores and libraries contact Small Press Distribution, at (800)869-7553, or on the web at *www.spdbooks.org*.